Love,
Dad

OTHER BOOKS BY JOSH McDOWELL

*HOW TO HELP YOUR CHILD SAY "NO" TO SEXUAL
PRESSURE*
*WHY WAIT? What You Need to Know about the Teen Sexuality
Crisis*
*TEENS SPEAK OUT: What I Wish My Parents Knew about
My Sexuality*
*EVIDENCE FOR JOY: Unlocking the Secrets of Being Loved,
Accepted and Secure*
*THE SECRET OF LOVING: How a Lasting Intimacy Can
Be Yours*
GIVERS, TAKERS, AND OTHER KINDS OF LOVERS
*HIS IMAGE —MY IMAGE: Biblical Principles for Improving
Your Self-Image*

JOSH McDOWELL AS SERIES EDITOR

Dating: Picking (and Being) a Winner
Sex: Desiring the Best
Love: Making It Last

Love, Dad

Positive Answers for Young Teens On Handling Sexual Pressure

JOSH McDOWELL

WORD PUBLISHING
Dallas · London · Sydney · Singapore

Love, Dad

Unless otherwise noted, all Scripture quotations are from
the New American Standard Bible (NASB), © The Lockman
Foundation 1960, 1962, 1963, 1968, 1971, 1973, 1975,
1977.

The Living Bible (TLB), copyright 1971 by Tyndale House
Publishers, Wheaton, IL. Used by permission.

Library of Congress Cataloging-in-Publication Data

McDowell, Josh.
    Love, Dad / Josh McDowell.
        p.   cm.
    Summary: Explains the physical and emotional aspects
of teenage sexuality and discusses the moral issues
involved in having sex or waiting.
    ISBN 0-8499-3127-4 : $8.95
    1. Sexual ethics for teenagers.   2. Sex instruction for
teenagers—Religious aspects—Christianity.
3. Teenagers—United States—Sexual behavior—Juvenile
literature. [1. Sex instruction for youth. 2. Sexual
ethics.] I. Title.
HQ35.M395 1988
306.7′088055—dc19   88-20541

Printed in the United States of America

89801239 BKC 98765432

Acknowledgments

I am deeply indebted to Paul Lewis for his time, talent and insight in shaping this book into being. He has not only been a trusted friend and co-worker for more years than I can remember, but a true hero and faithful father to his own children. I also want to acknowledge Joey Paul, Vice President, Educational Products Division of Word, Inc., who has pored over these letters and provided invaluable input. My thanks to Anne Wildman, editor at Word Publishing, and Dave Bellis, National Director of "WHY WAIT?", for their painstaking work to ready the manuscript. And ultimately, my thanks go to God, who has given me and my wife Dottie our four lovely children with whom I share these letters.

Josh McDowell
Julian, CA
May 26, 1988

Contents

8

1

A Letter from a Dad's Heart

Dear Kelly and Sean,

If books had arms,
this one would be
hugging you right now,

12

more strongly than any of the thousands of squeezes I've given each of you.

For the past couple of years you both know I've criss-crossed America speaking, appearing on radio and TV and talking to young people about their sexuality. You've been with me on some of those trips.

Tears have filled my eyes more times than I can remember as I have listened to personal stories guys and girls have told me. My heart has been broken as they have talked about how their lives have been messed up because they didn't understand or know how to manage their sexuality.

If there was ever a gift your mom and I want you, Kelly, and you, Sean, to have, besides spiritual life itself, it's the gift of sexual wholeness. And that can be yours if you make it through our world's mine field of teen sexual pressure without getting blown up emotionally. To help you make it, I'm giving you this book. It's sort of a road map, drawn from the best insights, experiences, tips, and secrets I've been able to learn.

I've put them together in the form of letters to you from my heart. These letters say it just the way it really is. I've also included some letters written by young people I have met over the years.

Do you remember a while back when we all spent a day together at the San Diego Zoo? (Who could ever forget the face that baboon made at you, Sean!) We had a great day, didn't we! And one of the things that helped make it great was something that's usually thought of as being very restrictive—all those black bars on the cages and the big walls around the animal compounds.

There were lots of moments when we thought we could have gotten a much better look by going past the barriers. But you know that if we had, it would have been terror, rather than more fun. The barriers were there to protect us from the animals and provide for our safety.

And truthfully, that's exactly why God put up some barriers in our lives. One area in which there are barriers that you are becoming aware of is sex. God's rules on sex are there to protect us from getting emotionally wounded and to provide for the maximum pleasure of our sexuality as we follow his guidelines. People do enter those cages and compounds at the zoo, but only after they've been trained in how to do so safely. Those people discover a thrill in working with those animals that we can't know just looking in from the outside.

That's a lot like the way it is with sex. When you understand God's purpose for it and enter its "compound" in God's timing, the experience that follows can be thrilling.

Kelly, I see you as a teenage woman who knows how to enjoy her beauty and her female feelings to the maximum. But it must be in ways that do not lure and trap guys into wanting to take advantage of you. I picture you saving yourself and your gift

of sex for one special guy. He's growing up somewhere in the world right now. He is the guy who
will capture your heart and give you the kind of
genuine love God has planned for you.

Sean, in my mind's eye I see you becoming a
teenage man who is as handsome and healthy as
they come. I see you as a person who enjoys his
physical strength and ability. And I picture you being mature and secure enough to brush aside the
pressures to be "experienced" before marriage. I
see you knowing how to have fun and entertain the
girls you date without pressuring them to share
their physical affections with you.

I see you doing this because you have discovered for yourself the genuine power of God's Holy
Spirit as a force in your life that makes wanting to
please God more important to you than pleasing me
or Mom or even your closest friends. And, Sean, I
promise that to the best of my ability, I'll always
model this kind of man for you.

Kelly and Sean, as your dad, I want both of
you to know that mere words can never express the
intensity of the love I feel for you. I know someday,
Sean, you'll understand just how deeply a father
can feel love for his son or daughter. And Kelly,
you'll know the unbelievable strength of a mother's
love.

Next to my love for God and your mother, I
love the two of you and your sisters, Katie and
Heather, more than life itself. And that's what this

book is really all about—discovering the jewel of true love and experiencing it for the rest of your lives.

I've told you many times that no mistake you could ever make in life could cause me to stop loving you. And it's true, because God's love is at the foundation of my love for each of you. The Bible is very clear that "In this is love, not that we loved God, but that He loved us and sent His Son to be the propitiation for our sins" (1 John 4:10). And just as you can't turn off God's love, there's no stopping mine either . . . no matter what mistake or choice you will ever make. But it's because I love you so much that I would like to see you make good choices and avoid mistakes if you can.

With both of you, Kelly and Sean, I've always had the honor of your trust and open communication. I realize that's probably going to be tested many times in the next few years as you become more your own adult selves. But in that process I want you to know something very, very important. There will never be anything you think about that I won't be interested in listening to you say. There will never be any question you can even imagine asking that I won't want to hear.

And that's not because I feel I have to know everything about you. It's because, after God and your mom, you are the best friends I have in this world. I want to talk and laugh and cry and struggle and serve and win with you for the rest of my life.

16

Well, dear Kelly and dear Sean, here are my letters to you. WOW, do I ever love you both!

—Dad

P.S.   It's OK with me if you want to share any of these letters with some of your friends who you think might find them helpful.

2

"Why should I wait until marriage?"

Dear Kelly,

I was so thankful
after our talk
the other night!

20

Your mom was too! We've worked and loved hard for seventeen years to build the wonderful marriage we enjoy. You've seen us, at our best and at our worst. And in spite of that, to learn that you want a marriage just like ours . . . that's about the best compliment we can imagine a marriage ever receiving.

After talking it over, however, Mom and I weren't sure you should want a marriage "exactly like" ours. Marriage involves blending two unique personalities. So, your marriage will obviously be unique and different in many important ways, because you're unique and different and the man you marry will be also.

What we do hope for, especially in the area of the physical, is that your sexual experience in marriage will be the best that it can be—like your mom's and mine. We're confident it can be because we know you are committed to sexual purity. It may be hard to understand why waiting until marriage before you have sex is so important to maximum sexual fulfillment. Let me try to explain. This may get a little deep here, but stay with me.

Remember last month when we talked and laughed about how much more interesting boys were becoming? All you knew was that what you were feeling was so neat that life would be a lot duller without it. Your new interest in boys is FUN. You have begun thinking about your body and theirs. That's OK. God meant it to feel that way. It is a natural part of the working of your body, the physical house He created for your spirit to live in.

The big problem we have, though, is as old as Adam and Eve. Do you remember, the first reaction that followed Adam and Eve's sin in the Garden of Eden was that they became ashamed of their naked bodies? Ever since, modesty (covering one's "private parts") has been an instinct among even the most primitive of peoples. But when two people have sex, it's more than just the clothes that come off. They also kind of strip naked emotionally. But we can't afford this kind of "nakedness" with just anyone. Do you know why? Because when we uncover ourselves emotionally, we are in danger of being emotionally wounded.

This is why sex is not like giving "a stranger" a handshake. Sex isn't that casual. The reason breaking up with someone with whom you have been sexually involved is so painful is that a lot more than your body is involved. It's not just your physical body that is being discarded. *You*, yourself, have been rejected, and all that you are and stand for.

Because sexual intercourse goes to the very core of who we are, it makes sense then, doesn't it, why God designed for sex to be enjoyed only within the boundaries of marriage. Marriage provides the protection of a lifelong commitment between two whole people, not just their bodies.

Think about it. You want to be seen as a sexually attractive person, but you want more than that.

22

If the physical sex act was all there was to it, prostitution would be the world's greatest job. But everyone wants more than just the physical. We want a deep, personal relationship. We want to be able to totally reveal ourselves to someone we can trust to accept and love us just the way we are.

Kelly, there's another reason Mom and I know that waiting for sex until marriage is so important. That's because it is spiritual as well as physical. The Bible points out that the two (husband and wife) become "one flesh" (see Genesis 2:24). Believe us, the best sex in marriage comes after prayer together. (Man is a spiritual being, so this makes a lot of sense.) Sex can affect us in almost the same way as knowing God does. God knows us all the way to our deepest being, and He loves us in spite of our faults. As I said earlier, having sex with someone means you "reveal" yourself at a very deep level. And then you are made humble, but also more secure, because you realize that your husband or wife loves you in spite of any faults they may discover in you. This is truly wonderful, because God blesses the sex act in a spiritual way and uses it to build us up emotionally. But obviously, this blessing would be missing outside the commitment and security of marriage.

Sex also involves your mind. Men and women aren't like animals. You remember when Carl's dog, Lady, was in heat. It was obvious that the sexual behavior we saw was simply animal instinct. No choice was involved. The fact that dogs aren't ready for sex all the time—just when their hormones kick in—shows you what I mean.

In us humans, sex involves our minds—our ability to choose. And because our minds and spirits are constantly involved (as are our emotions), sex is always very personal. It's between a man and a woman. And the relationship between them is never really the same again afterwards as it was before they had sex. When the time comes someday that you "give yourself" to a man, he will "know" something about you that can never be forgotten. And you will "know" him. In fact, this word "know" is the word the Bible uses to describe the sex act, as in Genesis 4:1: "Adam *knew* his wife." God wants sex to be the way a husband and wife say something very special to each other.

Kelly, this may be more than you wanted to know, but without understanding that sex is so intensely personal, the rules God set up to protect it might not make much sense to you.

I think part of the reason the idea of waiting until marriage for sex has become so unpopular these days is that there are so many unhappy marriages. The logical solution most people think of is to "liberate" sex, to separate it from marriage, so that it at least can be enjoyed even if there is no marriage commitment. But from what we know

24

about why God created sex, this would be impossible. And as hard as some people might try to change this, they never will.

My precious daughter, Mom and I were very careful about expressing ourselves sexually over the years before we ever knew who that special person would be that each of us would marry. There were a lot of moments when it was real tough to stay pure. But we're incredibly glad now that we did. It has given us a much easier path to experiencing all that God wants for us in this area. Every time we share sex together, we're sort of celebrating the vows we made on our wedding day and the unity we have on all levels—spiritually, mentally and emotionally as well as physically.

Kelly, you will be able to have every bit of this and even more if you walk close with Jesus over the next few years. It'll be each date and each relationship at a time until God brings a man into your life that is best suited for you to love for a lifetime.

You can count on our prayers, Kelly. We love you so much. It'll be a great day when that special guy shows up and we get a glimpse of how God is answering our prayers . . . and yours!

Love,

Dad

3

"What makes sex great?"

Dear Sean,

You "Hot Dog!"
Soccer wasn't enough,

you had to make the all-star team in baseball also. I'm really proud of you. I'm your biggest fan (next to your mother, that is). Just think, there's another whole batch of all-star teams for you to make when you hit high school in two years.

When I was in high school, I was both the mile run and the pole vault champion. I'll never forget when I went to the district championship track meet. It was the first time I had run against runners from larger schools. I was scared. When the gun went off, I thought I was in the wrong race. The other runners took off like they were racing in the 100-yard dash, not the mile. All I could think about as they passed me was the embarrassment of finishing last. However, one by one, they started falling behind and I won the third place medal that year.

Son, do you know what I miss most now when I think about those days (besides the thrill of competing)? It's sitting around the locker room laughing, playing pranks and telling stories with the guys. When the team won a meet or one of us did real well, the sense of friendship and feelings of unity were really fantastic. So, enjoy it all now, buddy, while it lasts. It ends too soon.

Of course, there's one thing I don't miss any more. And that's all the locker room talk about sex. From listening to all the talk it seemed like there was a lot of off the field "scoring," and that seemed to be the most important game to win. Let me warn you, Sean, that locker room talk can get pretty crude sometimes.

Some of the jokes are really funny, I admit, but you'll probably find out that saying "I love Jesus," and still laughing at some of that stuff just doesn't go together very well. Even just saying "sex is a beautiful gift" doesn't fit with the gestures and jokes about sex. Our sexuality is very important to us and something so potent should be treated with respect, the way God designed it to be.

But there's something far worse than disrespect involved here. The jokes and dirty language leave you believing a lot of wrong ideas and even straight out lies about what makes great sex. Besides the fact that a lot of the "information" you get is just not true, most locker room talk implies that all there is to sex is how many times, how often, and who with! But there is more to it than that, Sean. Much more.

For starters, although it's no big news, most people don't even realize that God is the one who thought up sex. The Bible says that it is God who made us "man and woman" (see Genesis 1:27). And that fact alone should give us some clues. Logically, the person who knows best how to help us get the most out of it, must be God. Funny, isn't it, how the popular belief is that God's somehow down on people enjoying sex. Nothing could be further from the truth.

It may be hard to believe sometimes, but what your mom and I are always telling you about the

purpose of rules, especially God's laws, is true.
God's laws aren't meant merely to limit what we can
do, but rather to *provide* something we truly need
and to *protect* us from the things that could hurt us.

True, one reason God made sex was so that
you and I and everyone else could arrive on the
scene—and what a way to get started in life, huh!
Let's face it, without sex, you wouldn't be here! But
there's another reason why sex between married
people is so great. And this is even more important.
Sex is God's wonderful way of allowing a man and
woman to express the depth and intensity of their
commitment to each other. And they do this in a
way that is so fulfilling and so loaded with excite-
ment that it never gets tiresome or boring. It just
gets better and better for their whole lives. God's
Word calls this closeness "becoming one flesh" (see
Ephesians 5:3).

It's true. That is God's plan. Sex, in a marriage
based on commitment and love, produces something beautiful for people to enjoy all their lives.
But outside of this special union—I mean marriage—people's sinfulness will always reduce sex to
something ugly and dirty. If you believe everything
you hear in the locker room, you will think that just
to have sex with anybody is fun. But even if this
were true, would you be willing to risk taking a
moment of "fun" if it meant you might lose out on a
lifetime of satisfying unity with your wife? Do you
want to give away a part of your emotional self that

you can't get back to a girl with whom you don't intend to share the rest of your life?

Sean, you won't hear about this in the locker room. But the truth that a lifetime commitment is what makes for great sex is the most important lesson you can ever learn in helping you to come out a winner in this area of sexual temptation. And this is one area in which you don't want to risk being a loser.

One more thing, son, unless you let them know differently, everyone's going to assume you think just like they do about sex. But your mom and I are pullin' for you to put together a winning game plan. Don't follow the crowd. In fact, a bunch of them will follow you if you express the confidence that you know where you're going.

Can't wait to see you play in the all-star game . . .

Love,

Dad

4

"Am I ready to start dating?"

Dear Kelly and Sean

Why should I be so lucky to have smart kids like you?

Yeah, I'm serious, you've got more savvy than I
ever did at your ages. I can see it in the question
you asked me: "How do you know if you're ready to
date?" Most teens want to know at what age they can
date. Like at 14? 15? But the tougher issue is how to
know if you are *ready.* Good thinking!

Well, let me answer by sharing with you five
questions you can ask yourself about dating that will
help you determine whether you are ready. Kids,
there's probably not one in a hundred of your
friends who've thought about dating like this. If
you're smart enough to press yourself for good answers, it'll really pay off for you. I found that these
really work!

1. Why do I want to date?

At first, that seems like a stupid question. The
obvious answers are because I want to, it's fun, all
my friends are and I want to join in . . . I want to
grow up . . . I want to experience love.

However, when you ask yourself this in light of
being a Christian, some more important reasons
come up. We want to accept and be accepted by our
date. We want to give and receive appreciation for
our own and each other's talents, gifts and qualities.
If you're thinking about growing up, there's probably no better way to "grow" than for these concerns
to become a vital part of your reason for dating.

If you feel you're not particularly interested in

these things yet, then socially you may be very
ready to date, but emotionally and spiritually
you're probably not mature enough to handle the
responsibility. You see, the process of dating involves more than just having a good time. It also
involves relating to another person in a meaningful
way, a way that will help each of you feel good
about who you are and about your relationship
with the other person. Dating is a relationship and,
kids, with every relationship there are certain cau-
tions and responsibilities.

2. What kind of person will I *not* date?

This question seems backwards, doesn't it? But
actually the word *not* helps focus on an important
issue. Will you date, even once, a person whose
moral convictions are significantly lower than
yours? For example, if you have decided not to
drink alcoholic drinks, will you go out with a person who thinks it's OK to just drink beer if an
older friend will get you some? Or, if you have de-
termined not to become sexually active before marriage, will you date someone who you know regards
sex as a game you play on a date? If you will, it
means that you are prepared to get into a situation
where there may be great pressure to compromise
your own standards. And if you do compromise,
you will probably look for reasons to justify yourself for doing so.

A mistake here may not nail you the first time or maybe even the first ten times. But, as sure as sin is sin, you'll eventually get burned. No one is immune. I have dozens of sad stories I've heard from young people who thought they were.

What's the point of risking a great failure and personal tragedy simply because you believe the lie that you're smarter than the average bear?

3. What are my physical affection standards?

Here's where your maturity or immaturity really starts shining through. It's easy to tell yourself, "Hey, I'm good and I'm not going to do anything foolish. But, I'm not a prude either, and I can at least enjoy myself. What's wrong with that?"

There's nothing particularly wrong with that, except that in a world which all the time promotes such a twisted set of sexual values, it gets real tough to think straight. Think for a moment. Would you know the difference between feelings of real love and feelings of infatuation? Most of the time when a song talks about being "in love," or someone in a movie or video is "in love," what they are describing or showing you is infatuation. Infatuation is that foolish feeling which is blind to the other person's faults and sees the relationship mostly in terms of what it can do for "me." Take a look at these differences.

Infatuation	Real Love
A. Physical appearances are very important. "She's a really cute chick," or "What a hunk!"	A. Physical appearances are not more important than personality.
B. Sexual attraction is constantly on your mind.	B. You like being with the person even when you aren't thinking about physical contact.
C. When together, you think a lot about kissing and making out. "I wonder what it would be like to . . . "	C. While showing affection is important, you're careful to be courteous and respectful and you enjoy doing all kinds of things together—from roller skating to working on school projects.
D. The other person hasn't any faults. "She's not being mean to her brother. That's what he *deserves* when he acts like that.	D. When the other person does something that bothers you, you recognize the problem and want to work through it.
E. You hide some of your faults, just in case the other person won't like you.	E. You want to be liked "warts" and all, so you avoid pretending and let your real self be known.

40

Infatuation	Real Love
F. You think a lot about the satisfaction the other person brings you. "All the other girls are jealous of me because Frank and I are dating."	F. Your real focus is on how happy you can make the other person.
G. One or two main things are what attract you to the other person.	G. You're attracted by many qualities besides looks, including similar life values and goals. "We both think many of the same things are important—like we're both Christians and want God to be honored by our lives."

4. How will I control my passions?

The dictionary says that a passion is "a strong emotion that has an overpowering effect." You've been overpowered by anger and lost your temper. Or been unable to stop crying because you were so sad. You may also have experienced, or at some time will, a "passionate" longing to express your feelings for your boyfriend or girlfriend. To be ready to date, you have to be ready to deal with what may become almost "overpowering" emotions. You're only in trouble with this one if you think the answer is simple. Passion, like forest fires, starts with a spark which, instead of dying out, grows and grows. And you'd better hope passion does work that way, because that's one of the reasons why making love over and over to the same man or woman a whole lifetime can be so satisfying. But controlling that passion outside of marriage can get tough for some people. Here's something I think will help.

Make a checklist for yourself like the one below. Some of these things may not apply when you first start going on occasional dates, I know. But as you get older it will help if you make these decisions before you begin dating regularly.

What will or won't you do?

YES   NO   I will not get into the back seat of a parked car with my date.

I will not be in my date's bedroom with the door closed.

I will not go inside my date's house if no one else is home.

I will not explore under my date's clothing.

I will not allow myself to press tightly against my date's body.

I will not go to movies or look at videos or magazines which I know will arouse me sexually.

42

YES   NO   I will constantly play this recorded
message in my mind: "I am keep-
ing myself for the one I will one
day marry."

I won't date a person who has a
reputation for easy sex.

It's never too late to start doing what is right,
but frankly, it's much easier to make these decisions
right at the start of a dating relationship. Once you
become too emotionally involved, it's harder to
make wise decisions. Probably one of the most important things you and your date can do is to plan
what you *are* going to do on your date—that way
you won't end up in sexual activity just because you
didn't have any other plans. So, be sure to plan your
dating strategy well in advance.

5. If I blow it, what will I do?

The answer to this one is more important than
you might think, because how you answer it reveals
your real attitude about what you've done. How will
you handle yourself if you compromise on standards
you set for yourself earlier? Your options are two:

1. You can admit you blew it and be restored
through honest repentance and forgiveness. Then
commit yourself again to pure standards. The Bible
says, "If we confess our sins, He is faithful and
righteous to forgive us our sins and to cleanse us
from all unrighteousness" (1 John 1:9). Or . . .

2. You can convince yourself that what happened in this particular situation wasn't actually wrong. "Maybe we got a little carried away, but we've been going together for months and after all, we didn't actually do it and lots of kids do." You excuse your actions and adjust your standard.

Sean and Kelly, besides being loved by God and learning to love Him in return, there's not a lot in life that's going to contribute to your happiness more than learning to love a special person and becoming skilled at nourishing your love relationship.

We aren't born with the skill. It's one we learn. And frankly, there's no better school than the home environment we grew up in (or a good one we've watched carefully). Dating is like the pop quizzes, papers, mid-terms and finals along the way. They reveal how much we've learned and whether we've mastered the course.

Both you, Sean, and you, Kelly, are smart enough to excel in your school work. Here is another area for you to apply your smarts. So, both of you, go for it!

Love,

Dad

5

"What do all these changes mean?"

Dear Kelly,

What a joy being your dad!
I'm so proud of you.

48

There are moments when you make me pop buttons with pride at what you accomplish. And last night was one of those big moments.

How lucky I was to be able to go with you and Mom to the science fair awards ceremony. I mean, Kelly, knocking off first place in your category for the whole county isn't bad! And then, receiving three special awards! That's quite an accomplishment. You sure put a huge effort into it, so I know you deserved the recognition you received. Way to go!

Something else caught my attention last night too as I watched you on stage with the other winners. On this flight to Denver this afternoon I just have to write you and tell you about it.

Sitting there watching you last night made it crystal clear right before my eyes that I was losing my little girl and in her place a very precious woman (and I hope lifelong friend) was emerging. I realized like I never had before the wonderful little changes that are taking place in what you talk about and what you laugh at. I don't know why it should come as sort of a surprise to me, Kelly, but you're truly growing up and I'm loving it 'cause I love you.

My thoughts didn't stop there, though, because I began to think about all the stuff I know life's going to throw at you in the next five years. And it scared me.

Honey, you're smart and doing a great job of growing up, but I thought I'd write to you about some of the changes you're experiencing. And listen, there are some incredible growing pains ahead which I know may hurt you like they did me. But every kid has to go through them. And I guess it's just the love I feel for you right now that makes me want to help you find the healthiest possible route to maturity.

Kelly, you're at that age now called adolescence. The feeling you must be having about now is, "I thought it would never come!" Well, it's here, and you're facing some super big changes that call for some super big coping, which can be super traumatic.

As a young adolescent, you're now going through that awkward physical stage called puberty. You already know some of what it's all about. Your body has started growing through some rather rapid and wonderful changes. Mom has already talked with you about starting your menstrual cycle, and all that.

Guys go through real changes too, like hair begins growing all over their bodies and they become much more muscular and coordinated.

The culprit in all this is this little peanut-sized gland with a big job, called the pituitary. Wow, it starts doing a number on us just before adolescence that yields awesome results.

Just for starters, you're beginning to find on your body all those feminine curves you've fantasized about, and in just the right places. You're discovering whole new feelings about guys, too, and about being with them and about what "turns you on" and what "turns them on."

Now, it may sound corny or simplistic, but seriously, Kelly, all this leads to another big part of adolescence—passion. I mean those good ol' deep, robust feelings of intense affection directed at boys who, not so long ago, you couldn't even stand to be around. Suddenly, both you and they have transformed before your very eyes. They're looking great!

For sure, it's no biggie to watch passion portrayed on TV or in the movies. But let me tell you, when you start feeling it yourself, there'll be moments when you're convinced that a new supercharged version of the stuff has been invented especially for you. It's powerful!

Now, all this could be sounding just a bit overly dramatic. But knowing the truth of what I'm saying makes me excited and scared for you, both at the same time.

The scary part, Kelly, is the way many adolescents act on those passionate feelings and then try to influence others to join them in their emotional forest fire. Believe me, I know. What I'm referring to is called peer pressure.

Let's be realistic. Just about everyone in your life, outside your family and a few mature friends, will begin expecting you to give wings to your sexual feelings and to experience it all now for yourself . . . more or less as soon and as often as possible. Most of the time giving in to these pressures may seem like the most obvious and logical thing to do. I mean, when Mom or I suggest some idea, your first thought is often probably going to be "Oh, no! Here it comes again. The big chill from my overly cautious parents who are totally out of touch."

Well, in reality, Kelly, I think I know you well enough to know that in the area of sex you want to save yourself for marriage. So, face it, you're going to be labeled a "virgin." And the pressure will be on for you to conform to your friends' standards concerning sex. This peer pressure may be some of the toughest you've ever had to face, because it will be a pressure to conform and it will be based on "the fun you're missing out on."

Kelly, when your mom and I were growing up, having the reputation of being a "virgin" was kind of a badge of honor really mature girls wore (and I guess guys too). The really sharp guys mostly wanted to be associated with girls who believed in saving their virginity until marriage.

Can you imagine? It's all so different now that such a thought sounds like it comes out of the dark ages. So it just goes to show how much values have been turned around by the messages we get from magazines, movies, TV, and also, let's admit it, so much of rock music. These big guns in our lives have ushered in a moment when kids your age can't remember when everyone wasn't bragging about their sex lives. Being a "virgin" (except when you're talking about the AIDS epidemic) now carries with it a stigma instead of a star.

Unfortunately, giving in is easy. It can be done before you even know what happened. And there are times even now when your mom and I aren't there to run up the caution flag and help you think it all through. You're on your own—alone, except for one thing. And it's a really big "one thing."

On your side you have your personal faith in the power of God's Holy Spirit to help you do the right thing. And that power is much more awesome than any peer pressure you will face. Take it from one who knows, you will remain the winner you are if you will consciously reach out to God when you are under pressure to do something that compromises your standards. His Spirit living in you will help you to cope. This saved me so many times I can't begin to tell you how important it is to stay close to God.

Well, the seat belt sign just went on and we're about ready to land, so I'm going to have to end this. I want to mention just one more thing, though. Your moving through adolescence is probably going to be as hard for your mom and me as it might be for you. You might feel that we are hesitant to give you the space you feel you need, and as a family we will struggle with that. But remember one thing:

Everything we do is because we love you so much and want to keep you from getting hurt.

Kelly, here's one person who has lots of confidence that when it comes to saying "NO" to sexual pressure, you're going to be the same winner you were at the science fair. Just remember that "the world's greatest adolescent" needs to watch out for the down side of the big three—PUBERTY, PASSION and PEER PRESSURE—and then you'll come through it all with flying colors.

Here is an approach I regard as a very mature and wise way of handling sexual pressure. A girl wrote me and said she was a 17-year-old virgin and a senior in high school. Her "sexually experienced" friends were pressuring her to become sexually involved and teasing her about her virginity. Finally she said to them, "Look, I don't want any more pressure about me becoming sexually involved or jokes about my virginity, because each one of you needs to realize that whenever I want to I can become like you, but you can never again become like me."

If this letter serves only to open a bigger or more important window of conversation between us over the next few years, I will be delighted. Talk back to me whenever you want, kiddo, I'm all ears!

Love,

Dad

6

"Is sexual curiosity good?"

Dear Sean,

It sure was fun sleeping on that boat together.

58

I hope someday we can rent a boat like that and sail for a couple of weeks in the Caribbean as a family.

Last night you really touched something deep down inside me with your honesty. All I can say is thanks for trusting me with some of the secrets of your heart, and for asking such blunt and candid questions about sexuality. I just hope I'm up to the task of responding. So, here goes.

You talked about the strength of the sexual passions guys feel inside, and sometimes those feelings become very strong indeed. There may come times when they will even frighten you, they're so strong. You'll sometimes feel like you're "a hormone with feet." Boys sometimes wonder why they can't stop thinking about those feelings. Sometimes it may bring on guilt feelings because Christians may have said that it's a sin to feel what you're feeling. Then, at other times, you will feel proud of what you feel inside because it all confirms that you are a normal, very sexually healthy guy.

You said you wonder at times whether girls feel passion in the same intense ways. And you're right in guessing that on a date if they did, at the same time as the guy did, controlling yourselves could be nearly impossible. You wondered if this is the reason why so many of even Christian guys and girls you know seem to violate the moral standards they've been taught. Sean, those are great questions.

I've got news for you. You're not alone. There's not a guy your age or older who hasn't wondered about these things. You're just better than most at being able to put your thoughts into words and maybe more honest than most in risking sharing your thoughts with your dad. Thanks.

Sean, God created our sexual feelings to be wildly wonderful and very deep. I've learned, however, that in the sexual area, just as in so many others, the ability to feel great pleasure also has its "dark side." It can also produce really bad results and serious damage and misery when it's abused. In James 1:14 and 15 there is a warning to Christians that "Temptation is the pull of man's own evil thoughts and wishes. These evil thoughts lead to evil actions and afterwards to the death penalty from God" (The Living Bible).

And, son, you asked a good question, "Do girls feel the same things?" As I have talked to young people over the years, girls have been very honest with me and said that they have sexual desires and feelings just as strong as any guy. And you can ask your mom about that also. Look, if that wasn't true, we men wouldn't have needed the blunt warning Solomon gave about the dangers of being tricked and lured to our emotional and spiritual deaths by a woman who doesn't have her sexuality under control. Check out Proverbs 7:21–27.

Sean, on my last trip to Virginia a college student traveled with me for a week. The second day of the trip, Jeff (that's not his real name) shared that he had made a big mistake in judgment when he

was just about your age. He sees now that if he had
been smarter, he could have saved himself a lot of
pain and spiritual struggle. So, here's what the
voice of experience, according to Jeff, now sees as
the real truth.

Jeff's first mistake was to decide he would try
to satisfy his growing curiosity about sex in the
same ways most of his friends were—by taking in
all the sex magazines and movies he could. He
fooled himself into thinking that this would be the
really "mature and healthy approach." He told himself that it was OK because he would get "an education," he would find out all he wanted to know
about women and about sexuality and his curiosity
would be satisfied. But not actually having "fooled
around" himself, he thought he could become wise
about sex without "sinning." That's what he thought
would happen.

But all Jeff really succeeded in accomplishing
was to fill his mind with lies and twisted ideas about
sex. What happened then was that when he *did* date
girls, his mind would picture trying to experience
what he had read about and seen. Rather than satisfying his curiosity, the "information" he had gained
from the sexual literature produced huge battles
with guilt. He sometimes felt like a boiling pot of
internal conflicts right during his date. Some kind
of fun person to be with, huh?

When Jeff finished his story, I asked myself
this question: "If I were in his shoes and had it to do

over again, how would I handle it?" Well, son I'd do three things.

First, I'd promise myself that no matter what I ever felt or did sexually, I'd find someone (like my dad or a mature friend or whomever) to be open with and talk to when I felt the need for information or to discuss something—someone other than my buddies who were themselves going through the same growing pains I was. You've already taken this step, with our talk last night.

Second, I'd get out my Bible and a concordance (or have someone who knows how to use a concordance help me) and look under all the headings like "lust," "passions," "fornication," and "fornicators," etc. Then I'd write out the verses which seemed to explain to me God's point of view, word for word, on 3 × 5 cards. If He's the one who thought up sexuality (and He is) then it just makes sense that checking the "owner's manual" to learn how it's supposed to work best would be very smart.

Sean, I'd stack all these cards on my desk and try to read through some or all of them once a week, or more often when I sensed that my feelings about sex were out of line with God's teaching on the subject. Or when I felt I was being controlled by some sinful sexual thoughts. Or after I had been exposed to a sex magazine or made a poor choice about a movie I had watched. Or if I handled myself badly on a date. I would go back to those cards to clear my head and regain God's views about sex (as well as His forgiveness if I needed that too).

Then, third, I'd write down on a piece of paper a very private note to myself. On the left half I would spell out the specific standards and commitments I felt I really wanted to keep and why. On the right side, I would write down the best plan I could think of for how to escape when tempted to sin in that area. When you're in the middle of intense temptation, clear, creative thinking is nearly impossible. But it's amazing how God will remind you of what you wrote down earlier as the way of escape.

Sean, probably the most important thing about handling your curiosity about sex is this. The most important freedom you have is your freedom to choose. You don't ever want to surrender this freedom because of peer pressure or anything else. It's your freedom to choose. When you exercise this basic power of choice, you can either accept as truth anything your friends might say or reject their powerful accusations as untrue. And as you do that, you are saying, in effect, "I'm important. I am the one who is in control of me, not them." Guys your age choose all kinds of ways to satisfy their curiosity about sex. And your friends may pressure you to join them. But remember, it doesn't take much backbone to run with the pack. In choosing your *own* way to handle this question, you gain genuine independence.

Sean, you made a choice to share with me and to ask some very honest questions. I want you to know that I value that and that you're a person with enormous worth to me and your mom and—far more importantly—to God Himself. Continue to use your personal power of choice to choose what's not only truly best for you, but what's right.

More importantly, protect your power of choice so that your friends, or the media, or the music you listen to, will not be able to steal your freedom away.

One other thing I want to share with you, Sean, that may help you in relating to some of your friends. Depending on their age and a whole lot of other factors, some guys don't experience the same intensity of sexual feelings as others. And there are guys who, at this stage of their lives, aren't very comfortable around girls and, frankly, just prefer to hang out with the other guys. Over the years, I have talked to many young men who went through this experience and they have shared that their greatest fear at that time was that they might be homosexual. As the years passed they soon realized that they were just as "normal" as the other guys! Some kids also like to toss the word "Gay!" around as an insult at guys (and girls) who just don't want to get sexually involved. Don't fall for that kind of emotional

64

blackmail, either. Keep your freedom and guard it well.

I love you, guy. And I'm really proud to be your father.

Love,

Dad

"How do I handle the 'pressure lines'?"

Dear Sean and Kelly+

You two are growing up so fast. It's such fun being your dad.

I so enjoy our time together and all the "new things" we talk about. One of those things is the new interest both of you are having in the opposite sex as a group and as individuals you find attractive in a specific way. I was thinking about this when I received a letter from a former classmate in college. His oldest daughter Ann (18) sent a letter to her younger sister Julie (16). Ann had gotten some ideas from my book *Why Wait?* that she wanted to share with her sister and she included them in her letter. I asked permission to share the letter with both of you. Even though you are a bit younger than either Ann or Julie, I thought it might give you some things to think about. Here it is.

My dearest sister Julie,

A couple of days ago Mom sent me the snapshot of you and Ron leaving for the dance on your first date. What a cute couple you were, and what a hunk he is! I hope you had a fabulous evening. I'm so happy for you!

Between the lines in Mom's letter, I could sense she and Dad were a little nervous about it all—just like I remember them being about my first date.

It's strange, but looking at that photo flooded my mind with a lot of memories of *my* first date and dance. Would you believe, I found in my album a photo of me and Ralph (my first date) that Dad took of us standing at exactly the same spot in the living room!

That seems like such a long time ago. I can't believe it's been just four short years. Realizing that made me know that I had to write to you . . . and now!

Julie, I can remember thinking and feeling that Ralph fulfilled every fantasy I ever had about the guy I would love to love. He was cute, popular, really smart, a star on the varsity basketball team, and he didn't do drugs and wasn't into alcohol. We were even in two classes together. When he asked me to go with him to the dance, I just couldn't believe it.

We dated for about six months. Do you remember the way you used to tease me about marrying him? I'll never forget the embarrassment I felt and how mad I was at you. Maybe now you can begin to understand what I was feeling!

Looking back, I realize I didn't truly understand what I was feeling either. And I sure wish I had.

Precious sister, everybody holds "love" up as the official banner and motto for playing the dating game. I think the word "pressure" is probably much closer to the truth. The pressure to conform and to perform started when I was dating Ralph and it's never let up. I don't know a girl here at college who feels any differently than I do.

If you aren't already feeling plenty of that pressure, you're going to, and that's why I've got to warn you about what I've learned the hard way.

70

Maybe you can learn how to handle it better than I did.

My confusion about what love really is started on that first date with Ralph. Everyone always said he had great hands as a basketball player. It was probably true, because from the very first date his hands were all over me! And while a part of me loved every minute of it, there was another part of me that gradually grew very confused and even frightened, really.

I was loving the popularity of being Ralph's girl too much to love myself like I should have. So, I just kept burying the fears inside me and pretending it was all wonderful.

Guys are very clever, Julie. Some of them can come up with a million arguments for why you should give them the physical and sexual favors they want. I'm going to give you an important advantage in what can be a war by telling you the pressure lines in advance, so they won't take you by surprise. Listen carefully, and get prepared, because the next time you hear these, it may be in a situation where you will least want to resist. The lines are all designed to help you easily give away two of your most valuable possessions—your purity and your self-respect.

"You'll let me if you love me," is one of the oldest. The real truth is that if the guy loved you instead of lusting after you, he wouldn't ask. If the relationship is one you care about keeping, you won't give in to his false argument. Because after you've had sex, it'll be impossible to feel good about going back to holding hands. "Let me prove how much I care for you," is another way of saying the same thing.

"I want to make love to you." Julie, this is the lie of the century—that love is the same as sex. Sex may eventually follow where there is genuine, committed love, but it's hardly ever the other way around. And you won't be the exception, I promise you.

Another common line is: "Everyone's doing it." The pressure here is to be considered popular and in step. "What are you afraid of?" is another way guys say this one. It's become unpopular these days not to be "experienced." But the pressure to be part of the "in" group never recognizes the future joys it will take "out" of your life at the same moment— the joy of being able to give yourself, in a unique way, to your marriage partner.

"Just try it once. If you don't like it, we won't do it again." Something as valuable as sexual satisfaction isn't for casual testing and experimentation. It's real love and commitment that make sex more than what a couple of dogs do on the front lawn. And when there's no marital fence around the relationship, it may feel physically good at the moment, but the aftertaste will be very sour. By then it's too late to get back what you traded away in the "test."

"If you turn me on, you have to follow through," is a really twisted up thought. Some guys can be turned on by just about any woman. So watch out for this false "compliment." (At the same time, in fairness to the guy, be sure that you are not behaving in a way that is likely to "turn him on," either unintentionally, or deliberately to satisfy your own ego.)

"Sex is a natural thing to do . . . like being hungry or thirsty. It's no big deal." This is plainly untrue. So, when you hear this one, simply respond, "Well, if it's no big deal to you, then you won't mind if I say 'no.'"

"You don't know what you're missing." This certainly seems true on the surface, but the subtle lie in it is the argument that I should experience everything there is to experience so that I won't miss something. Skydiving may be one of life's most thrilling adventures, but I don't have to rush out and skydive today just because I might be missing something. There's a proper time and place for everything.

Julie, there are more "lines," but I think you can see what I'm getting at here. They're all just ways to pressure you into having sex before you should, and into spoiling for you what should be one of your greatest pleasures for life. Don't give in, little sister. And if you hear a new "line" from some guy, add it to this list and tell me what it is. We girls have to stick together.

I love you so much!

Ann

8

"What are some reasons why I should wait?"

Dear Sean,

What a great job you did on your report about Zimbabwe.

76

I'm glad you and Johnny were able to work on it together. I admire your persistence in finding the right material, especially in finding the ten words in one of the Zimbabwean tribal languages, and their English translations.

Sean, when you take health at school you will probably have to do a report on some aspect of human sexuality. One topic you could work on would be positive reasons to wait until marriage for sex. You may think that's a subject you're not ready to consider yet, but I want to encourage you to think about it, even now.

In this connection, I was asked by Mrs. Gilbert, the health teacher at Poway High School, to put together material about defense against sexually transmitted diseases for her to use in her sex education class. This has become a very hot topic, and a lot of research is needed in light of what's going on. The information I have uncovered is frightening. But authorities are agreed that the *best* defense is monogamy (sex with only one person).

Son, let me share with you some of the best of the material I have collected. The "reasons to wait" cover a lot more than just defense against AIDS and other STDs, however, and they sure made a lot of sense to me. I hope this will help you personally to sort out your thoughts in this area. It's so easy to let your feelings rather than your mind decide some of these things.

Here are most of the reasons I listed for Mrs.
Gilbert:

1. Premarital sex makes the rest of a relationship more difficult. The time you spend together
becomes focused on the physical. This prevents
your relationship from growing in the area of discovering who each person is, what each personality
is like, and developing a real friendship. Outside of
marriage, the genuine communication upon which a
mature relationship should grow is lost while the
couple concentrates on the phony substitute. These
other areas are far more important to a successful,
lifelong relationship than sex. And in fact, if you are
aiming for great sex in marriage, they are the real
foundation on which it will be based.

2. Premarital sex takes away the specialness
of sex in marriage. When both partners entering
a marriage are virgins, there are none of the scars
or emotional baggage to be overcome. In fact,
premarital sex is like a thorn on the rose of free
sexual expression in marriage until the partners
can forgive each other and receive God's forgiveness as well. This is especially true when one partner enters marriage as a virgin and the other does
not.

3. Premarital sex decreases self-esteem. Self-
esteem is how much you believe in yourself—how
much you like yourself. At first, a sexual relationship can give you a false sense of being accepted,

feeling special. But you feel a sensation of being let down as you realize this is a lie, and this feeling can take years to overcome. It can really hurt to find out you were "loved" only for sex, or that your relationship had nothing else going for it than sexual attraction.

4. Premarital sex leaves deep scars. "Love you forever" feelings, which convince some couples that premarital sex is OK, don't last forever. Sex is always a giving of some special part of yourself. And when a couple breaks up, that part which was given becomes lost—never to be regained. This emotional scarring is very difficult to overcome.

5. Premarital sex leads to unwanted pregnancies and abortions. No method of birth control is 100 percent effective, especially in the inexperienced hands of young people. So the pregnancy that only happens to other people happens to you. An abortion may seem the simple way out. But remember, number one, it is killing another human being. And secondly, research reveals negative long-term effects, mostly for the girl, but they may also involve the guy.

   81 percent can't quit thinking about the aborted child.

   73 percent have flashbacks to the abortion experience.

   69 percent experience feelings of "craziness" after the abortion.

54 percent struggle with nightmares related to
the abortion.

35 percent have visions or dreams of visitations
from the aborted child.

23 percent experience hallucinations related to
the abortion.

72 percent say they had no religious beliefs at
the time of the abortion, but 96 percent in
retrospect regard abortion as the taking of
life or murder.

6. Premarital sex leads to possible comparison
in marriage. Sex should get better and better as a
marriage matures. But if one partner comes into the
relationship with "experience," he or she will usually
have flashbacks or draw comparisons to previous experiences. If there is any lack of fulfillment or enjoy-
ment during the time it takes for the two partners to
learn how best to please each other, these comparisons can lead to serious sexual difficulties. The emotional problems between them that can then result
are one great way to ruin a marriage.

7. Premarital sex tears down trust. Marriage
partners who know their spouse didn't save sex for
marriage often struggle with doubt about whether
or not their partner will be faithful inside marriage. Confidence and trust become more difficult
to maintain (and these are the foundation stones of
a good marriage). In Proverbs 20:6 the Bible asks:
"Who can find a trustworthy man?"

8. Premarital sex can lead to sexual addiction. When a sense of the purity and specialness of sex is lost, it can lead (as with other emotional cravings) to abuses and addictions. Sexual addiction is never healthy and always produces more abuse, pain and personal destruction.

9. Premarital sex destroys freedom. The big lie is that freedom means doing what I want, when I want, with whomever I want. In reality this is lawlessness, not freedom. Sexual relations involve two *people*. People are much more than just a physical act. And their actions impact all the other people each partner is related to—family, friends, etc., and even future spouses. It is only within the security of the commitments and promises of marriage that you can preserve real freedom of sexual expression.

Son, I hope these "reasons to wait" help you understand why the Bible says, "This is the will of God . . . that you abstain from sexual immorality" (1 Thessalonians 4:3).

If you do a paper on this in the next couple of years, I have a lot of current information on STDs—sexually transmitted diseases. Even if the other reasons I have listed seem a bit removed from where you are now, the stuff I have dug up on STDs would strike a holy terror in anyone's heart about experimenting with sex outside of marriage—including your own.

I'd love to see whatever paper you decide to

do. Knowing your gift of pursuing research you'll do great. And I and the rest of the family will be applauding you.

Go get 'em, son. I'm proud of you.

Love ya,

Dad

"Is there such a thing as 'safe sex'?"

Dear Kelly,

It is late and
you are asleep.
What a joy to
see you growing up.

You are in a wonderfully exciting stage of life right now.

Lately I've been involved in a research project for another book. It deals with how to help kids understand why God says to wait for sex until marriage, something we have talked about before. I wish every junior high and high school kid I know could meet some of the couples I have interviewed in my study. Some of their relationships are scarred by some very real (and very painful) experiences which I think any smart person would rather learn from now than repeat later on.

This one couple, however, Steve and Sharon, have been going together for almost two years. They're truly in love. They both know it but they're putting off marriage talk for a while. They both want to get through school first.

When they began realizing that their dating relationship could go on for another couple of years, that applied some pressure about how they were going to handle their physical relationship. Sometimes the pressure to express their love sexually really gets to them. Both of them have been taught, as your mom and I have taught you, that sex should be saved for marriage. Nevertheless, at times they are attacked by doubts why they should, when they love each other so much and expect one day to be married.

Well, I was trying to think of something that would help them and I got this idea of them interviewing a group of unmarried guys and girls on the campus about their views and experiences on all this. I proposed that it would make a great term project for Steve's clinical psych class. The professor thought it was a good idea, so they've been talking to all kinds of people,

Kelly, you're really cute and will certainly have plenty of opportunity to be sexually active if you want. And it'll come a lot earlier than when I was your age. Honey, the stories Steve and Sharon heard the past couple of weeks are really distressing. I want to share some of them with you. Maybe this will strengthen your will and commitment to wait even more, like it has Steve and Sharon's.

Listen to what Steve and Sharon have been told . . .

"I fell in love with a girl two years ago. We dated a few weeks before any real talk of sex entered our relationship. Both of us were very open and honest with each other about sex. We spent the rest of the spring and the following summer "experimenting." Before entering college that fall we both decided to have sex. We did. Our relationship began to lose something from then on. We tried sex again to try to make up for the loss, but God's gift of sex became empty and sickeningly automatic, unreal. After almost five months of anxiety, emotional pain and deep frustration, we broke up.

"It's been more than a year now since the months of anguish and hell. Even with the forgiveness and love of Jesus I am still hurt and scared inside. Jesus heals the pain and gives me a genuine sense of forgiveness, but the memories remain.

"Fornication is a deeply personal kind of sin. It involves your very being: mind, body, heart and soul. Paul wrote in 1 Corinthians 6:18, 'Run from sex sin. No other sin affects the body as this one does. When you sin this sin it is against your own body' (The Living Bible). I know exactly what Paul meant. I hope sharing this experience will help someone else to not make my mistake."

*   *   *   *   *

"Someone asked me if I was still a virgin. I wanted to be cool, so I said no. Now that people have that in their heads about me, why should I wait?"

*   *   *   *   *

"Sins against God lead to ugly consequences. In the case of my girlfriend and me, premarital sex not only scarred us individually, but also damaged our relationship and ultimately hurt others outside the relationship.

"At the beginning I used premarital sex to deal with the fact that I didn't like myself very much. Because my partner was not always willing, I saw those times as a chance to talk her into it, to control her, and to be accepted by at least one beautiful girl. Each time we had sex it proved to me that I was a man and gave me good stories for the locker room. I looked to premarital sex to make me feel OK instead of looking for worth in the eyes of my Creator. When my girlfriend became pregnant, I hated myself even more."

*   *   *   *   *

"My girlfriend and I first had sex when we were fifteen. I'd been going with her for almost a year, and I loved her very much. She was everything I wasn't—friendly, outgoing, popular. We'd done everything but, and then one night she asked if we could go all the way. A few days later, we broke up. It was the most painful time in my life. I figured sex was the problem. I had opened myself up to her more than I ever had to anybody, even my parents. The next year I went to high school. I was depressed and moody and nervous. My friends dropped me because I was so bummed out. In junior high, see, I'd been the star football player. I had better things to do. By high school, I felt like a failure. I wasn't in sports any more, I didn't exactly look like a movie star, my grades weren't terrific. When I was seventeen, I had intercourse again. A bunch of guys I knew went to a girl who was sort of a slut. That was awful, too, fast and frustrating. I felt like I had malfunctioned. I'd read those things in *Penthouse* magazine about how some guys go all night, for hours. I wondered if other girls—girls I really like—would hear about it and say I was a lousy lover. I didn't go out with a girl again until I got to college. I've had mostly one-night stands in the last couple of years. I'm afraid of falling in love."

* * * * *

"I had dated this one guy for about six months before we decided to 'go all the way.' When I first met him I really hated him, but after I got to know him better, I started liking him and eventually grew to love him. During our relationship I accepted Jesus into my heart. However, I continued seeing this guy and it didn't take long for me to get away from God. At first I had felt we should quit sex, but as Jesus said in Mark 14:38, 'The spirit is willing, but the flesh is weak.'

"So we kept having our relationship and I got farther away from the Lord. Pretty soon it was like I was getting little warning signals from God saying, 'Come back to me. This isn't the way for you.' But I kept on, and things got worse. This guy's feeling for me began to diminish; we saw less and less of each other; there were more signs of him using me. Finally after a great tragedy in my family—six people were killed—I turned and gave my life back to God, and this guy and I broke up."

* * * * *

"I recently broke up with a guy I'd been going with for over a year. After we had gone together for about six months we went all the way. At that time, we had plans to marry sometime in the future. We thought of ourselves as responsible because we used birth control.

"We did it a couple of times a month for a couple of months until one time we got too carried away and forgot about using birth control.

"The next month was terrible for me. I was so scared I was pregnant that the situation began to affect my grades, my nerves, everything.

"My relationship with this guy continued for a few months more until I finally tired of him and we broke up. This was really painful for me because of what we had done. Painful memories of this relationship haunt me now and these memories will probably not go away for a long time to come."

*   *   *   *   *

Kelly, it doesn't take a genius to figure out what the voice of experience is saying. Premarital sex is eventually trouble for anyone and any relationship. There aren't *any* exceptions.

For a contrast, listen to what Steve and Sharon heard from a young married friend of theirs:

"I know the temptations of premarital sex—the physical desires, the emotional desires, the peer pressure, and all of the good excuses. I was teased through high school and over two years of college about sexual abstinence. At one time I was even accused of being a lesbian.

"Then God brought Chad into my life. We knew we were going to get married, but we continued the struggle to refrain from premarital sex, through a fourteen-month engagement. I am now 23, and after three years of marriage I have never regretted the times we said "no" or the reasons "why not."

"I firmly believe that waiting until after the 'I do's' to experience sex has only enhanced our marital relationship. It has established a trust that cannot be equaled because Chad and I both love the Lord, and loved our prospective spouses so much, even before meeting each other, that we both wanted the first time to be with our partner for life."

Honey, I wanted you to read these parts of Steve's paper. You may want to share them with a friend or two . . . whatever. There's just one more thing I want you to know. You can talk to me about your feelings and questions on all this any time you want. I promise I'm unshockable. And you know, Kelly, how much I love you.

Love,

Dad

10

"What do I do with temptation?"

Dear Sean,

The other night when
we were talking,
it sure was fun

trying to answer all your questions. Or, should I say, trying to satisfy all your curiosity?

That evening brought back several great memories. It reminded me of those bedtime stories about Curious George. We used to read those stories so often, I think we must have worn the cover off every one of those books.

You know, I still think the fascination we had with the trouble that curious little monkey got into, helped turn you kids into persistently curious people.

In fact, Sean, I gotta tell you, I love it that you have such a wonderful and intense curiosity. You were always asking me and your mom and everybody about everything from internal combustion to how hair grows.

That curiosity will be one of your greatest strengths—the stuff scientific breakthroughs and great adventures are made of. And, buddy, you've got it coming out of your ears.

But, like most great strengths, curiosity also has its dark side. A lot of kids your age have discovered this. And you could get clobbered by it too. Sean, in the next few months and years your sexual curiosity could become one of your greatest enemies, as it did for the guy, Jeff, I told you about.

Now, don't get me wrong. It's a winnable battle if you're prepared. But you've got to know how. If you get through this stage of growing up with a healthy sort of sexual curiosity, it will be a fantastic gift when someday you marry a woman you want to love for a lifetime.

I know you're committed, like I was, to saving sex for your marriage. But, wow, it's so easy to be caught off guard. Passionate feelings and intense curiosity will so easily seep into your mind at the very moment when you're trying your hardest to control those urges and sexual thoughts.

So, Sean, I'd like to share some tips on handling sexual curiosity as the pressure increases to be sexually active. This may not be perfect, but it's the best advice I've got.

First of all, take a tip from all the ol' cowboy movies you've ever watched—head sexual temptation off at the pass. In this case "the pass" is the lie that comes dancing into your mind just when your guard's down. It's saying to yourself, "just one look" or "just one touch" won't hurt me (to see what it's like so I won't be an uneducated nerd). If this has a familiar ring, just think back to the deceit of that old serpent in the Garden of Eden.

The book of Proverbs warns about pressure to be sexually active: "With her many persuasions she entices him; With her flattering lips she seduces him" (Proverbs 7:21).

Sean, I don't know what you've felt inside so far, but once you get your sexual motor started and running, shutting it down is like trying to stop a super tanker. (Did you know one of those things takes miles to stop after you apply the brakes!)

God made the sex drive so that one thing automatically leads to another. That's what makes it possible to have great sex for a lifetime with your wife. The curiosity pays off there.

Here's another tip, Sean. Find a few friends to hang around with who share your values. Talk with them seriously about this area of sexual pressure. When you've got some guys who share your beliefs and who you can talk with honestly, the moral strength you gain from it will amaze you. Handling your sexual curiosity and passions will get amazingly easier. You know why? Because you'll be with people who are giving you approval ratings for being moral, rather than for being immoral. You can all support each other when you're feeling weak and your resistance is down. And low resistance happens to everyone.

I have here in my notebook a theme paper a student wrote on sexuality for his English class. He quotes a girlfriend of his who said:

"If everyone is having premarital sex and talking about it, your conscience becomes numb and you no longer feel the conviction against it. In fact, your friends encourage it. You begin to feel the pressure after so long. If you're a girl, the other girls make you feel that you aren't very attractive and aren't worth much and if you're a guy, the guys make you feel like a wimp because you're not experienced like others. After so much of that, you say, why not do it? Even though you know it's wrong, peer pressure overrules. At that point, you lay down your morals and turn your back on God's commandments."

Sean, I've got to go, but let me say just this one more thing. You know I'll never put you down, no matter what question you want to ask or whatever happens to you as you grow up and mature in this area. I know your mom would love to help too. Tough questions deserve to be answered. You don't ever have to be embarrassed about any question you might want to raise. I promise you, I'm unshockable.

You won't hear this very often, but being able to manage and control your sex drive proves a whole lot more about your true manliness than letting those drives run you wild trying to express them. You have heard me say many times that our most important sex organ is our minds, not our "plumbing." The plumbing almost always works. It doesn't require testing. It's what you've got control of in your mind that shows your maturity as well as your manliness.

Any guy or girl can flaunt his or her misuse of sex. It takes real guts these days to save it like a very valuable diamond until you find just the right setting where it can be displayed in all its dazzling glory. And that setting, of course, is marriage.

Sean, I didn't know I was going to write you

100

and Kelly a "book" on handling sexual temptation, but I'm glad I did. With curiosity like yours, I can promise you the battle will likely be furious.

You're a super son. Stay close to Jesus and keep doing yourself proud! You and that woman you'll one day marry will both be glad for the rest of your lives.

Love,

Dad

11

"How far is too far?"

Dear Sean,

You said yesterday that it's neat (I think you actually said "rad") to have a youth speaker for a father. There aren't too many kids who have their own private in-house counselor, right?

Well, I like having a "rad" son like you too. But, listen, I'm not so sure about playing the role of in-house counselor. The question you asked me is not all that easy to answer, but it is a classic:

"How far is too far?" in being physical with girls you date. At first glance, the question seems a little like asking "How big is big?" or "When is enough enough?" You're not the first guy, or girl for that matter, to struggle with that question. And the answer you come up with will automatically answer many of the questions that follow. It will also help you keep your head clear when you're flying high in the thin air of romance.

Son, everyone is different. We're different spiritually, physically and emotionally. And that's why it is often so difficult to draw conclusions in this area for someone else.

Nevertheless, as a starting point, I know you have a desire that Jesus Christ be Lord of your life in this area too, so we should begin by looking to the Bible for advice. It's interesting to me that beyond the clear warning against sexual intercourse outside marriage, there isn't much else written in Scripture on this subject. That's not surprising, however, because at the time it was written, Jewish men and women hardly saw each other before marriage. The opportunity for anything sexual to happen just wasn't there—even casual sexual contact, and certainly not petting.

Petting these days gets defined a lot of different ways. But just so we both know what we're talking about, let's use the term to refer to touching the breasts and genitals. But even within this definition there's a lot of elbow room. Touching a girl's breast through her clothing is a lot different than lying naked together. And concerning various specific actions like these outside marriage, the Bible is silent. Nothing is said there about holding hands, kissing, hugging, French kissing, or any of the other things we would call sexual activity. All these things fall into sort of a grey area.

What I know you're looking for, and what everyone wants, is for someone with "authority" to step up and draw a hard and fast line and say, "OK, everything up to here is fine. But you can't go past this point as a Christian without violating God's will. It sounds nice and simple, but the reason it doesn't work for everyone is the fact that people are different and react very differently in the same situations. Some action that is very sexy to one person may create only a mild reaction in another. This is especially true in the sexual response differences between guys and girls.

A girl, for example, may simply receive a pleasant feeling from brushing up against a guy, while the effect on the guy could be to get all kinds of wild thoughts going through his head.

So, in all honesty, there's no magic line up to which you can go racing, dangle over, and be perfectly free as long as you don't fall.

Actually, the better question to ask is this one: "How far should I or we go?" What are those honest, caring actions I can use to show my true feelings to my date? What actions honestly express how much I care about and am committed to my date at this point in our relationship—not, what would satisfy my desires at this time? It's not so much "How far is too far?" but "What is honest, righteous and best for where we are right now?"

I used that word "righteous" on purpose, because if there was ever a single guideline that could safely lead you in almost every situation, it's simply this: You can happily share all those physical contacts which don't raise desires in either you or your girlfriend which cannot be righteously fulfilled.

Do you understand what this means? I know this is difficult to get at, but let's say a couple is touching or kissing and it's causing either of them to want to move on to something they know God wouldn't approve of. Or they know their actions would lead to frustration in the relationship, especially in the emotional part. If this is the case, no matter how "beautiful" the feelings seem to be, that action can't be "right."

To work out what this means in real life, let's consider several things, one at a time:

The first is the issue of getting in touch with your own (and your date's) emotions, passions, and the reasons why you do things. It usually starts so slowly that you don't realize it's happening, but when either one begins to raise their own desires above what is right and spiritually healthy for the other person, they've crossed an important "line."

A second issue is to apply the basic biblical commandment to "love one another" to the situation. We're not talking sex here. We're talking the 1 Corinthians, Chapter 13 kind of love which unselfishly seeks out God's very best for a brother or sister in Christ. Before that girl you're dating is anything else—friend, lover, or whatever—she is a child of God and special and precious in His sight.

Then the third key issue is to recognize that the reason physical affection between a guy and girl is so exciting is because God made it to be that way. It's a basic drive, although it's not a basic need. And it is progressive in nature—one stage always naturally leads to the next.

Recently, Sean, I helped a high school girl figure out a chart on this progression. It was a project for their sex education class. I think that you'll find the diagram we made up is as interesting and helpful to your thinking as she did. Here it is:

The Road to Sexual Arousal and Intercourse

Abstinence

N		
e		Holding Hands
c		Hugging
k		Casual kissing (peck kissing)
i		- - - - - - - - - - - - - - - - The Line
n		Prolonged kissing
g		

L	P	
i	e	French kissing (including last
g	t	stages of necking—ears, neck)
h	t	Breasts covered
t	i	Breasts bared
	n	
	g	

H	P	
e	e	Genitals covered
a	t	Genitals bared
v	t	Oral sex
y	i	Genital to genital
	n	
	g	

Intercourse

Now note that I've drawn a line labeled "The Line." You wanted an honest answer to "How far is too far?" Well, for whatever my personal opinion is worth, here it is. I don't believe most healthy Christians in a dating relationship, whatever their age, can progress much beyond this point without asking for trouble. If you and your date are honestly committed to saving sex for marriage, you need to realize that past this line you begin to arouse in each other desires that cannot be righteously fulfilled outside of marriage. That gets us back to that standard again.

Let me point out right here one more key point in this progressive nature of physical expression. It's often overlooked. And this is the factor of time. If you spend a lot of time with a girl you enjoy being with, your relationship will grow to the point where you feel more and more comfortable expressing yourselves more and more physically with each other. This happens even if you aren't really moving along the progression chart from one stage to the next. This is important to remember, especially if you and your date are too young to be even thinking about marriage, or even if you are older but have several years to wait before you can get married. Remember that the further you go through the progression, the more difficult it is to slow down or stay at that level.

So, Sean, it's important for you to realize that you need to make a decision where you personally

will draw the "line" in your dating relationships.
Otherwise, you may easily find that you wind up
doing some things that you would never have believed you could possibly do. And that decision
needs to be made at a moment when you are thinking clearly about this whole question, long before
the passion hits.

If you've already set your standards and
"drawn your lines," that's probably the only way
you'll be able to make your commitment stand up in
a situation requiring some serious resisting. You
won't end up making a mistake you'll later regret.

I know you've heard it said that Christians
should never date non-Christians. This advice always tends to sound kind of rigid. But its value lies
right here in this same principle—the progressive
nature of physical and sexual attraction. Any guy/
girl relationship that has a real chance of getting beyond say the first meeting or date, also has a chance
of moving all the way to a marriage commitment.
Face it, you'll never marry someone you didn't date
the first time, and the second, and so on.

So, OK, son, let's apply this to the situation you
may be facing quite soon:

You're a young, attractive, healthy guy. You enjoy, as you should, the way girls are attracted to you
and you to them. You want to fit in with your
friends (as much as your Christian beliefs will allow)
and be "one of the guys." You are looking for a
magical line that you could put up to help you know

"How far is too far?" Sean, you can seek advice, as you've wisely done. But in the end, the decision is really yours, and whether you will live by the advice will depend on the strength of your commitment to Christ and the presence of the Holy Spirit in you. You see, if you are growing in your relationship with Christ, and learning more and more about Him and about what the Bible teaches, asking yourself the question, "What would Jesus do?" will give you guidelines for behavior. This will enable you to really enjoy yourself in your dating relationships and to walk through them without constantly feeling like you're having to buck the rules and limits. You know, as I do, that the Christian life is a living relationship with Christ, and not an exercise in religious rule-keeping.

So you see, if we are walking close to Jesus, the question is no longer: "How far is too far?" or "How close is too close?" If you and your girlfriend are both consciously committed to honoring God in your relationship, the door is wide open for you to go into the relationship and for both of you to grow in exploring it as far and wide and deep as you want. In other words, *you* will be making the decision of how far you should go, based on your love for Christ and your honest caring for each other, and bearing in mind what you have learned about the progressive nature of sexual activity.

Well, son, I hope I've been some help. I love you so much, guy, as a son and as a good buddy. I'm so proud of the excellent qualities I see emerging in you as you mature, now more rapidly than ever. After you've read this and have given these ideas some thought, maybe a heart-to-heart talk about it all can fill in some of the cracks and round off some of the edges. I'm ready.

Love,

Dad

12

"Can lust be controlled?"

Dear Sean,

Hey, what a fight!
Your description of that
heavyweight title bout

was fantastic. Wish I could have seen it with you. It should have been billed as "the fight of the century." Sean, in the next few years, you are going to fight a real "heavyweight" fight as well. I'm talking about the battle with sexual temptation that every guy faces during his teen years.

I've never talked about this with you before, but even I as an adult still have to protect my mind from temptation. I think every man does. There's no foe more vicious than lust. I admire your maturity in being willing to talk about this subject, and if anything I can say here will help you get on the right track, it will have been worth the effort to write this letter.

Let me give you some of my key thoughts. Sorry, this may get to sounding like a sermon part of the time, but believe me, it's coming straight from the heart of a dad who, just as much as you do, desires more than anything to be pure and pleasing to God. Listen, if I say these ideas work, it's because I've put them to work in my own life.

For starters, let's recognize two amazing things: Most people these days have grown so used to lustful thoughts and feelings that they don't even see them as a problem and certainly feel no guilt over them. Our world basically says, "Sex is a natural appetite. When you feel hungry, feed it!"

The other thing which goes hand in hand with this is that we often don't talk much to each other about having lustful thoughts. It is rather refreshing to discover that Scripture talks a lot about it. Nothing's brushed under the rug there—the Bible's completely realistic.

So, what really is lust? I am convinced it's any sexual thought or action that might lead to disobedience of God's laws or could possibly hurt other people. I use the words "might" or "could" because real sexual sin begins back there somewhere in our minds as a "harmless" sexual thought.

Sean, you and I have heard many times the command in the Bible to "flee youthful lusts," but just what does that really mean? When you think about it, why would a loving God give us the ability to feel such a powerful force as lust and then command us to flee from it? There are two answers, really: First, lust is actually the "dark side" of love. Love as God designed it has all the same strong feelings as lust, but it seeks to build people up rather than tear them down. Lust turned up as the "dark side" of love because of man's fall, way back in the Garden of Eden.

Second, we're told to flee because lust is like a thief. It tries to steal our heart away from what God wants to be our first love—Himself. When you're battling lust (or giving in to it) your feelings toward God usually lessen. You don't feel His presence as strongly as you did before. And it's hard to regain this closeness to God as long as you keep excusing yourself for your lustful thoughts or actions.

Hey, it's simple. Lust is blinding and binding.

When we're enjoying our lusts, we don't see where it's taking us. Sexual lust (really planning to or actually having sex outside of marriage) *blinds* us to God's purposes for us and *binds* us to being a slave to our own feelings.

Now, Sean, on to the other big issue. When you want to flee, how can it be done—successfully? This is the last question on the Million Dollar Pyramid. But the answer is so simple that it's usually overlooked.

Sean, when you're struggling with lust and giving in regularly to the temptation, honesty will gradually disappear from your spiritual relationship with God. You may still be reading your Bible. You may even continue to pray or go to church. But the real genuine honesty in your prayers or your serious desire to apply God's Word to your life or having a true sense of worship when you go to church is just plain missing. It all becomes a habit rather than a relationship. It's kind of like the difference between the first burst of intense love you feel for a girl you've just starting going steady with and the feeling right before you break up. At the end of the relationship you're just going through the motions.

So, bottom line, when you renew the honesty and vitality of your relationship with God, you will start winning again the battle with lust. It works because to genuinely feel love for God always leads to wanting to please him. And that leads to obedience. The one always follows the other. But renewing your relationship with God requires a deliberate decision on your part—a decision to *be* honest with God in your prayers, and to try to respond honestly and obediently to what you discover in reading your Bible.

There's one other important truth here, however, Sean—and that is that just keeping a warm walk with God won't automatically guarantee that your bouts with lust will disappear. Jesus Himself was tempted in the wilderness and there will be "wilderness" times in our lives as well. The important point is how we respond to them—especially in this area of sexual lust.

I've got to bring this to a close, but here are some practical principles to help you handle sexual temptation:

1. Your body is a spiritual battlefield. So, get used to the idea that the war there will continue until Christ returns.

2. Take responsibility for your actions. The big lie that really tricks us is the one that says that sexual urges are instincts beyond our control. It may be true of dogs, but it's only as true for humans as their twisted minds believe it to be. Most of the time we get into bad situations because we *choose* to get into them.

3. Control your thought life because this is where lust begins. There's no way to do this outside filling our minds with God's Word. Here are some scriptures that can help: Psalm 51; Proverbs 6:27,

28; Romans 6:12–14; 1 Corinthians 6:9–11 and 10:13; James 1:12 and 4:7; 1 John 4:4.

4. Choose your friends carefully. Make sure they are people who are going to *help* you, not make it more difficult for you to handle temptation. This gets back to the issue of choice. It's yours alone to make.

5. Don't get overconfident about lust, but don't get overfearful, either. Both extremes are dangerous.

6. Confess your struggles and sins to God as well as to another Christian you trust. Talking openly can protect you from fooling yourself, and what a blessing that can become.

7. When you see or meet a girl who brings lustful thoughts to mind, force yourself to look into her face and especially her eyes. This will help you to recognize and respond to the real person that is there and not just the body that person is living in.

Well, Sean, I warned you this might seem a bit like a sermon, but when it comes to overcoming battles with lust, you gotta go for the truth and tactics that really work. These truths have been field-tested. You will be safe with these weapons, my not-so-little son. Pray for me, and you can bet I'll be doing the same for you.

Love,

Dad

13

"Is a fresh start possible?"

Dear Kelly and Dear Sean,

You both know how Mom
and I pray for each of
you that by God's strength

you'll be able to save yourselves sexually for that very special person you'll one day marry. So the letter that follows is one I hope will never apply to you.

But, if it should happen that you fail and make a big mistake and miss that goal, this will become the most important letter you will ever read. That's because it answers the biggest questions that you will be asking:

—Will Mom and Dad still love me as much as before?

—Will God forgive me and make the guilt go away?

—Can I get my virginity back?

Happily, there are positive answers here to every one of those questions. The intense pain you would experience while discovering them for yourselves, though, is one I hope neither of you will ever have to deal with. I love you!

This is a letter that was sent to me recently, kids. I got permission to let you read it. However, I changed the names.

Love,

Dad

P.S.   If one of your friends should fail to "wait," this would be a great letter to share with them.

Dearest Liz,

I love you, sister! I know how scared you must feel right now, but I LOVE YOU! I LOVE YOU! Can you hear me? I'll write it here ten times bigger if it will help you believe me—truly I L-O-V-E Y-O-U!!!

The fact is that you've made a mistake, and a big one, and have done what we promised each other we would never do—surrender our virginity before marriage. But that's not going to change our relationship! There's no way. A mistake, no matter how bad, just doesn't change the fact, sis, that I still love you with all my heart—as deeply as before—and more now than ever!

You ask, "Am I sad?" Yes, of course. I cried for a long time after reading your letter. And I admit that I am feeling the disappointment—and probably even some of the anger you are feeling. For sure, I'm panicky like I know you are about whether you're pregnant. Not knowing yet, the waiting must be very scary, and I'm praying so hard for you.

I think you know, sis, that right now prayer is the one thing you can do. It's really the most important thing we both can do.

The timing of your letter was amazing. Would you believe the topic of my Bible study last week was "forgiveness"! And right now, whatever the outcome of your pregnancy test, I know your greatest need is to experience God's forgiveness. You need to know that He can and will wipe away your sin. In fact, He'll forget it forever, even though you and I will still be able to remember.

Liz, will you promise me that the moment you know the results of the early pregnancy test you'll call me? Promise? Please do, so we can talk! I can cut a couple of days of classes and come home to be with you. Really! It's not that far and it would be OK. I know this is not the kind of thing you are ready to talk to Aunt Susan about.

Right now, what I want to say is so important, so please listen and truly hear me. I'm sure this is exactly what Dad and Mom would be saying if they were here. It's one of those moments when it's especially hard not to have them around.

There are all kinds of ways to approach the problem. And different people will see it differently. But when you get to the basics, I believe that God sees it as sin. That may sound very scary for you, but the wonderful part about seeing the problem the way God does is that we can also find the perfect cure. When we sin and blow it and are truly sorry, God offers the only solution that works— forgiveness. His reason is as simple as it is amazing. He wants to continue the close relationship with you He made you to enjoy.

The important thing I want you to know right now is that I forgive you and God is ready to forgive you. You may not yet feel ready to forgive yourself, but God is ready. Remember those words in Romans 5:8? "While we were yet sinners, Christ

died for us." It's so important that you realize that
the penalty for this specific sin, in addition to all
the others, was paid for by Christ on the cross two
thousand years ago. That's so that right now, when
you confess your failure, you can experience a genuine release from guilt. From God's point of view,
it's over! Done! Finished!

Liz, I know you well enough to know that if I
were standing with you right now, you probably
wouldn't want to look me in the eye. I'm sure you'd
feel too ashamed. And believe me, I understand. If
we traded places, I'd feel the same way. But if I
could reach up from this page and turn your face to
mine and look into your eyes—tears and all—you
would know that I accept you and I have already
forgiven you.

Actually, that's the same reason you can look
me, yourself, and God, in the eye right now and
smile. It's because you are a forgiven and "free"
again person. No one is keeping score.

Dear sister, do you realize where your sin is
right now? It's at the bottom of the deepest sea. It's
as far from you as the east is from the west (read
Psalm 103:12). That's how real and full Christ's
payment for your penalty is. And you're really not
even allowed to go get the sin and bring the guilt
back if you want to. God has put up a "No Fishing"
sign. It's off limits.

Oh, I know what you're thinking right now:
"Yes, Sidney, but what if I'm pregnant and all that?

128

Forgiveness won't change that possibility. And also, I won't become a virgin again. So why is forgiveness so special when I can't get my virginity back anyhow?" But you see, that's why it's all the more important that you have God's forgiveness and can begin enjoying His fellowship again. With God, *whatever* the results of the pregnancy test, you'll have all His power and strength available to you to help deal with both the test result and your relationship with David.

I don't know what you and David may need to do. You may need to break off the relationship, or drastically change the ways you choose to express your love to each other. Should you keep seeing the same kinds of movies? Or go to the same places? Or keep the same group of friends? I don't know the answers for you, Liz, but please consider these questions carefully.

Sister, I believe you're truly sorry for what you did and that you'll ask for God's forgiveness. So, let me say again how important it is that you forgive *yourself!* I know you pretty well, and I bet you'll tend to forgive yourself only after you've been so hard on yourself that somehow you might think God owes you the forgiveness. Don't do it!

I'm not with you right now, Liz. So all I can do is say this: Please don't keep kicking yourself a thousand times an hour for what you have done. It's done and it's past. You can't change that any more than you can erase God's complete forgiveness.

Just as certainly as I'm writing this, Satan is going to try to make you *feel* guilty and unforgiven. But, Liz, because you know Jesus Christ as your personal Savior, you are no longer condemned. Romans 8:1 says it best: "There is therefore now no condemnation for those who are in Christ Jesus."

It's true, your physical virginity cannot be restored. Once it's lost, it's lost forever. You can't go back and change the physical fact. But your spiritual and emotional virginity *can* be regained. Romans 12:2 says, "Don't let the world around you squeeze you into its own mold, but let God remake you so that your . . . mind is changed."

When you and David made your mistake, your mind had been squeezed into the world's way of thinking about sex and love. Now the only way to be cleansed to the point of emotional virginity is to let God *remold* your mind from the inside. I think this happens this way.

You begin by filling your mind with *His* truth about people and about life from the Scriptures. Liz, if there ever was a time when I'm sure the Bible is going to mean a lot as you read it, it's now. So, take full advantage of this opportunity.

And remember that it's God's Holy Spirit who will show your heart and mind what the Bible means. He makes it a day-by-day living reality. So get ready, you're going to experience God's presence in a brand new way.

Another way your mind can be renewed and

your emotional virginity given back will be through the love and forgiveness you feel from other Christians. You know, even though I'm your natural sister, Liz, I'm also your sister in Christ. In fact, that's really the more important relationship between us. And you know how deeply I feel love and complete acceptance for you right now. That's God's love too, coming through for and to you.

Elizabeth, if you're not in a quiet, alone place, why don't you go to one before you read any more of this letter.

OK, what I want you to do is to visualize Jesus Christ standing beside you right now. He's saying to you these words from the Bible, His own words to you and me: "If we confess our sins, He is faithful and righteous to forgive us our sins and to cleanse us from all unrighteousness" (1 John 1:9).

"And when you were dead in your transgressions and the uncircumcision of your flesh, He made you alive together with Him, having forgiven us all our transgressions, having cancelled out the certificate of debt consisting of decrees against us and which was hostile to us; and He has taken it out of the way, having nailed it to the cross" (Colossians 2:13–14).

"And their sins and their lawless deeds I will remember no more" (Hebrews 10:17).

My dearest sister, you are so important and precious to me. As you make the right responses to your really hard situation, you will experience one more great thing from God. This one is His amazing ability to take life's worst things and turn them around for good. Isn't that the simple message of Romans 8:28: "And we know that God causes all things to work together for good to those who love God, to those who are called according to His purpose."

Do you remember that later in that same eighth chapter of Romans, in verse 35, Paul asks the question: "Who shall separate us from the love of Christ?" Then he lists tribulation and distress and persecution and famine and nakedness and peril and the sword as possibilities. I think in the same spirit, he could have listed "premarital sex." And if it were there, Paul's answer in verse 37 would still be the same: "But in all these things we overwhelmingly conquer through Him who loved us."

Sis, I hope you can feel God's love and mine coming through in all this. I'm not very good at teaching or preaching or whatever, but I am good at loving—especially you!

I can't remember ever doing it like this before, but why don't we pray together right now, just as if I was with you.

"Dear Jesus, You know my dear sister Liz's heart, and how scared she feels right now. And how sorry she is for stepping outside your will and having sex with David. Together we thank you for dying for this sin, and for forgiving Liz. I thank you that right now you've forgotten her sin and buried it in the deepest ocean.

132

Jesus, please comfort my sister, and put your peace in her heart about the outcome of the pregnancy test, whatever it may be. I know you're going to walk with her, both to help her control her sexual passions in the future, and even through a pregnancy if that's going to happen. We're going to depend upon your promise to make everything work together for good, for those who love you. Lord, we certainly love you deeply right now.

And Jesus, please help Liz as she talks with David to communicate accurately her feelings and to make clear the commitments they must act on in the future. Turn this experience into an important spiritual growth time for David, too.

Lord, Liz especially needs your resurrection power in her life right now. Help me to do and say the things she needs most. We're both so grateful that we can turn to you at a moment like this.

We've prayed and asked for these things together in the name of Jesus. Amen."

Liz, I'll be waiting for your call real soon. It'll be a special time for both of us.

Love,

Sidney

14

"Why are mistakes so painful?"

Dear Sam,

Hey, good buddy,
it was great being
in Florida with you.
I'm glad

you stayed with me while Mom and your sisters visited Grandma and Grandpa. It was neat just the two of us roughing it together.

Frankly, Sean, there's some stuff on my mind —important stuff—that has finally pushed me to drop you a line, because it really can't wait until I get home again.

Son, you and I talked briefly about some of the things we saw students doing on the beach in Fort Lauderdale. Some of the things that happen on Spring Break can not only be wild, but wrong and painful.

I've been thinking about what we said and would like to add a little bit more for us to think about together. I only wish I had had a father to level with me like I want to with you. If I would have listened, it could have saved me some real pain. So, I hope you've got your ears on, because that's why I am writing this letter.

There's no doubt about it, Sean, SEX IS A BIG DEAL! It's the bottom line to just about every joke, movie and magazine rack you encounter. It's on the mind of most of your buddies, and most of the girls at school. No surprise here—sex is "hot!" It's hot enough to deliver someday on every healthy dream you'll ever have about it, and hot enough also to burn and scar you for a lifetime (if you discover too late how to handle it). That's the part I'm going to tell you about—what the movies, music and magazines always leave out.

Sean, you know I care a lot about you, so here are some thoughts I hope you'll take to heart now that your formerly "puny" body is rapidly becoming anything but.

You met a guy this last week in Florida. I'll call him Greg. That's not his real name. Greg has "made it" with at least three girls. With his good looks, they just seem to form a line.

The rest of the story, however, isn't so romantic. Greg shared with me that a couple of weeks ago he was lying awake sometime in the middle of the night because he realized his past was catching up with him. He was trying to fall asleep after coming in from a date with this girl, Susan. They've dated eight or ten times. He had been telling me that he was really interested in her as a "person" more than a "body." But the date that night had just ended with them having sex in the back seat of the car.

About two hours later Greg was in real emotional pain—I mean deep stuff. We talked and he spilled his guts out to me. I have his permission to share what he said with you and I am going to do that because I don't want you to ever have to feel and say what Greg is experiencing.

Since junior high school days (about the age you are now) Greg's good looks and friendly personality have always given him an edge with girls. Dating just about anyone he wanted to was easy. And he learned quickly how to get all the physical favors—French kissing, hands inside the blouse, and all that. Without him realizing it, this became Greg's way of proving to himself and all his friends he was a man—maybe more of a man than any of the rest of them.

The trouble is, Greg now realizes that sex with a girl doesn't prove anything except that he has no self-control. He believes now that he has no ability to keep a relationship going for any reason but a physical one. He's scared that if he doesn't learn to do it differently, he's doomed to the same kind of a hell-on-earth marriage that his mom and dad had. (Greg's dad was always "cheating" on his mom. They're divorced now.)

Greg said he knew that there was something different about Susan. She seemed interested in him as a person and not "Greg the stud," and that impressed the socks off him. And while she was pretty enough (no beauty queen), he was attracted more to her wit and intelligence than her looks. Greg says they talked three hours straight on their second date, completely missing the movie they were supposed to go see.

What was tearing Greg up inside was that in his desire to know Susan better and be more open with her, the only thing he knew to do was to get physical, so he pressured her to have sex with him. Now it has ruined their ability to talk the easy way they used to. It has put an ugly barrier between them (because Susan is sorry she gave in). The great thing they had going has become a great mess.

Sex is "the proof of love," according to just about every message we get from the world around us. In truth, for Greg it has become the source of deep emotional pain. There is a thick wall keeping him from what he knows he needs and wants a lot more—real acceptance and love.

Sean, there's a powerful lesson in this for both of us. Like Greg, before I married your mom I had plenty of opportunities to "perform sexually." You know about one or two of them. Believe me, the temptation was great, even overwhelming at times. It would have been so easy to have bought the lie and gone that route. But the trade off for just one or even for a bunch of great moments of sexual passion just wasn't worth it. The test of a true man is that he has self-control. He has the power to save sex for his marriage relationship where it's protected by commitment before God. Only then can it work the kind of real magic that keeps on satisfying forever.

I've said all this very frankly, Sean, because I love you. I don't want to see you get hurt or hurt others. Some of life's lessons just aren't worth learning the hard way. You've got a couple of great coaches in your mom and me. So please try to let us in on your life in this area.

Well, I can't believe I wrote a letter this long.

140

Just goes to show you what true love can accomplish. I really do love you!

Love,

Dad

P.S.   I found these "love tests" in something I was reading the other day. They contrast love with lust and they're pretty good. As you start becoming more and more interested in the girls you are in contact with, you may want to stick this list on your mirror to help you keep focused on what's real. Maybe they'll help *you* think straight too.

LOVE	LUST
Love is forever	Lust is for now
Love is giving to another	Lust is getting for me
Love is tender	Lust is tense
Love is priceless	Lust is cheap
Love is patient	Lust is impatient
Love satisfies	Lust demands
Love makes you what you want to be	Lust makes you what you don't want to be

15

"Why is it so hard to talk to my parents?"

Dear Kelly,

How're you doin', kid?
Great, I bet. You've
always had a knack

for magically pullin' things out of the hat when life gangs up on you. Boy, what a talent! Where was I when they were passing that one out?

Seriously, I'm writing because of something wonderful that went on between your mother and me and it involved you. You had gone to Kristin's house and we were talking about you (relax, it was nothing bad). What we were discussing was how quickly you were growing up and how deep our love is for you and for your brother and sisters. Actually, I guess we talked as much about ourselves as about you—I mean about how we were doing as parents. I wish you could have been listening, it was so interesting. And much of it nearly brought tears to my eyes, because there was such honesty in our questions and doubts.

One question we asked each other was, "How would Kelly rate us as parents, if she were being perfectly honest?" Kelly, you know we're concerned because we don't want to lose good communication with you, as often seems to happen when kids reach your age. Maybe you'll feel like shutting us out sometimes because of some of the conflicts we might have over who and when you can date, and so forth. But, if you don't mind I want to reveal a couple of the things I'm learning about communication at my ripe old age of forty-eight.

Hey, this job of being real and truly open and revealing about ourselves to each other may be one of life's hardest things. And I guess from what I know, it's as difficult for dads and moms as it is for kids. No, I sure didn't reveal to my dad and mom a lot about what was going on in my life . . . especially after I started dating. But, I believe now that that wasn't such a good strategy—especially when it came to stuff like sexuality and dating.

So, what am I saying? Just this: Think seriously about keeping the window of communication wide open to me and your mom about your date life and your close friendships. There's a good reason I say this. Two forty-plus-year-old parents may know a lot more about "where it's at" than you might give us credit for.

Kelly, I read some recent research which showed that while 81 percent of parents believe they're getting mostly honest answers from their kids in conversations about sex, the same kids report that they are totally honest with their parents about sex less than 30 percent of the time. I think a lot of this may happen because some parents don't actually care what their kids do. Your mom and I aren't in that group. We're committed to tripling the 30 percent average.

As I've been thinking it over, I'm convinced the number one reason kids choose not to be open with their parents is that they fear rejection by the parents and the guilt that goes with it. Simple, isn't it? When we feel that what we are thinking or have done is different from what our parents expect of us, we clam up and stop talking.

I've often wondered why kids respond that way to their Christian parents. I don't think it is that they really disagree with the standards they teach. For the most part, they agree, as you probably do with your mom's and my standards. But in addition to not wanting to displease their parents, kids often feel like they need to express their grown up selves by not letting their parents know what they are doing. Kids don't want their parents looking over their shoulders, to keep them from making "mistakes."

Kelly, even though I know we have a good relationship, you'll probably have some of these feelings, too. That's OK. But please remember, communication is the key to a happy home and to getting along with your mom and me. If you accept that, the next question is, "Is there any one key to good communication?"

I think that there is, and I think it is this: *How* you communicate is a lot more important than *what* you say. Research is showing the actual words we use make up only about 7 percent of the total communicated message. The other 93 percent involves our tone of voice (38 percent) and non-verbals (55 percent).

This becomes pretty easy to believe when you think for a minute about how quickly you or I read those non-verbals (facial expressions and body language) or how our non-verbals are read by others even before we speak. It's like we believe what we see before we believe what we hear—even if the two messages are different. Interesting, huh?

So this is the point. For communication to improve, it has to start with focusing on *how* you say things to each other, more than *what* you say. Sure, it remains important both to speak the truth, but (even as Paul instructed in Ephesians 4:15) we are to "put off falsehood and speak truthfully" to one another, yet do it "in love." It's the "in love" part that makes it happen—that's the how part.

The trouble begins on both sides, doesn't it, when we stray from gut level loving and caring about each other. If we get focused instead on our rather petty individual differences and surface issues, communication stops. We must keep our eyes on the importance of the relationship rather than all the facts and details.

Well, daughter, I guess I got kinda technical there. Anyhow, I started into all this because I asked myself the question why you or I might not be able to talk freely about sexual issues. Let me conclude by sharing a simple "action" version of what I've tried to say here. See if it would make sense to try this. (Now, give it a try once before you laugh):

1. Start any discussion with us where you think there's going to be stiff disagreement between us by

making an up-front speech like: "We may not be able to agree on your answer to the question I'm about to ask, but I want you to know that if you don't see it my way, that's not going to diminish my love and respect for you. We'll just agree to disagree. And even if we exchange angry words, I'm going to hug you before I walk out of this room. OK?" Hey, that'll blow us away!

2. In the middle of the conversation, when you begin feeling you aren't really being heard, just stop and say so. Try not to clam up and leave or raise your voice louder and louder in anger in an effort to put your point across.

3. Make a promise to yourself that no matter what you're going to say to us it will be exactly what you think. It will also help if you can avoid "dressing things up" in a way that might talk us into agreeing with you.

Kelly, this may sound sort of wild and impossible. Maybe it even seems a bit lopsided in your mom's and my favor. But I know it'll work because of one key thing—your mom and I already want it to. Honey, you can bank on it. We're absolutely dedicated to having a healthy relationship and open communication with you, just as we seek to have that with each other. And wow, Kelly, it doesn't get any better than that.

Well, I gotta close this and get ready for a talk. I started this by praising your magical ability to pull solutions to life's problems out of the hat. You'll do yourself an enormous favor by using some of that magic right now to apply what I've said and open up fresh new communication with your mother and me. We're ready and you'll love it!

Love,

Dad

JOSH McDOWELL is one of the most articulate and popular youth speakers today, having spoken to more than seven million young people in seventy-four countries. A graduate of Wheaton College and a magna cum laude graduate of Talbot Theological Seminary, he is the author of twenty-eight books, and has been featured in twenty-one films and two television specials. Among his most popular books are *Evidence That Demands a Verdict, The Resurrection Factor, More Than a Carpenter,* and *Evidence for Joy.* His film series, *Evidence for Faith,* is a classic in the field of popular apologetics. Josh has been a traveling representative for Campus Crusade for Christ for twenty-five years, heads the Josh McDowell Ministries international organization, and is resident instructor at the Julian Center, a campus in the mountains near San Diego, offering a unique three-month discipleship experience. Josh and his wife, Dottie, live in Julian, California, with their four children.